Blood and Circulation

Jackie Hardie

RIGBY
INTERACTIVE
LIBRARY

© 1997 Rigby Education
Published by Rigby Interactive Library,
an imprint of Rigby Education,
division of Reed Elsevier, Inc.
500 Coventry Lane
Crystal Lake, IL 60014

Interiors designed by Inklines and Small House Design
Illustrations by Oxford Illustrators, except: Peter Bull Art Studio, p. 4 (left)
and pp. 22–23; Garden Studio/Darren Patterson, p. 27.

Printed in the United Kingdom

00 99 98 97 96
10 9 8 7 6 5 4 3 2 1

Library of Congress Cataloging-in-Publication Data
Hardie, Jackie, 1944 –
    Blood and circulation / Jackie Hardie
        p.   cm. – (Body systems)
Includes bibliographical references and index.
Summary: Describes the heart and blood and their functions, also discussing blood types,
pacemakers, the immune system, and ways to keep your heart healthy.
        ISBN 1-57572-097-3 (lib. bdg.)
        1. Cardiovascular system – Juvenile literature 2. Blood – Circulation – Juvenile literature.
[1. Circulatory system. 2. Blood. 3. Heart.] I. Title. II. Series: Body systems (Crystal Lake, Ill.)
QP103.H37   1997
612.1 – dc20   96-27552
                                                                          CIP
                                                                          AC

Acknowledgments
The publisher would like to thank the following for permission to reproduce photographs:
Corbis/Bettmann/UPI, p. 26; The Mansell Collection, p. 21; Oxford Scientific Films, p. 25 (bottom);
Science Photo Library, p. 5, p. 6, p. 7, p. 9, p. 11, p. 13, p. 17, p. 18, p. 19, p .20, p. 23, p. 25 (top), p.29;
Tony Stone Images, p. 28 (right).

Every effort has been made to contact copyright holders of any material reproduced in this book.
Any omissions will be rectified in subsequent printings if notice is given to the publisher.

Note to the Reader
Some words in this book are printed in **bold** type. This indicates that the word is listed in the
glossary on pages 30–31. This glossary gives a brief explanation of words that may be new to you.

Visit Rigby's Education Station® on the World Wide Web at http://www.rigby.com

Contents

The Heart and Blood

Blood is the body's delivery and collection service. It delivers food and **oxygen** to every part of the body, and it collects waste products, particularly **carbon dioxide.** Blood circulates, or goes around your body, about 2,000 times a day. It is pumped by the heart through tubes called **blood vessels.**

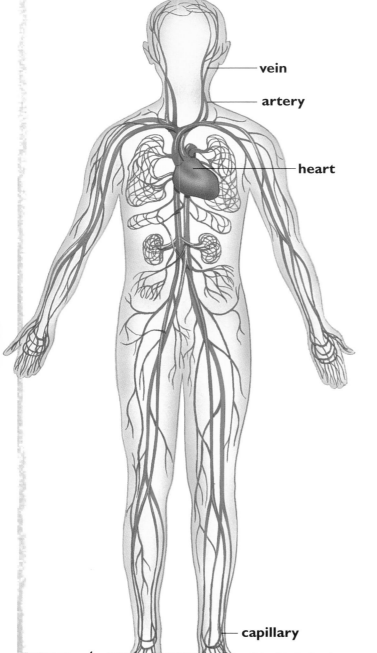

vein

artery

heart

capillary

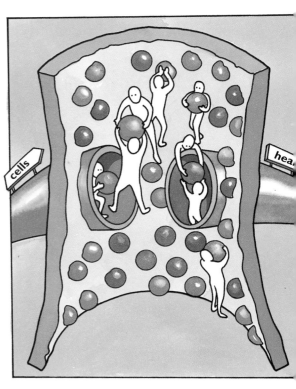

cells

hea

▲ Blood is a collection and delivery service for each **cell.** It brings food and oxygen and collects waste.

◄ The heart pumps blood to every living cell. **Arteries** (shown in red) take blood to different parts of the body, and **veins** (shown in blue) take it back to the heart..

Cells

Every part of your body is made up of millions of tiny **cells,** too small to see except through a microscope. Each kind of cell has a different job to do. All cells need oxygen, food and other chemicals to stay alive and do their jobs. Blood brings food and oxygen to each living cell in the body.

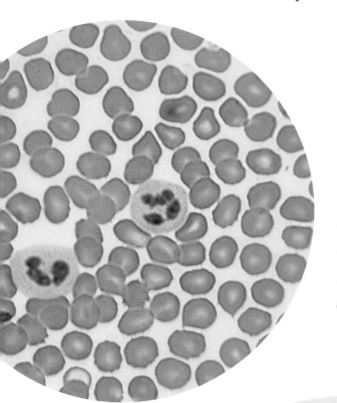

As each cell works, it uses oxygen to burn food to get energy. In the process, the cell gives off carbon dioxide. Blood carries this waste carbon dioxide away from each cell to the **lungs** where it is breathed out.

Moving things around

Blood travels away from your heart in blood vessels called **arteries.** Arteries branch into finer and finer tubes called **capillaries,** which spread out among the cells. There, food and oxygen pass from the blood into the cells. The blood continues its journey through the capillaries to blood vessels called veins. These take the blood back to the heart. Blood travels in only one direction around the body; it is a one-way system.

▲ *Every part of the body is made up of cells, even blood. Here, a smear of blood has been magnified about 500 times to show the different kinds of cells.*

Did you know?

There are more than 49,000 miles of blood vessels in your body. The biggest one is an artery which is about an inch wide and carries blood from the heart into the body. The smallest blood vessels are finer than a single hair. If all your blood vessels were laid end-to-end, they would stretch twice around the world!

Blood

When you cut yourself, blood oozes out of your wound. Blood looks like thick red juice, but it is really a yellow liquid called **plasma** with different cells floating in it. Plasma is mainly water with **blood proteins** and food **molecules** dissolved in it. If you smear a drop of blood onto a thin layer of glass and then magnify it with a microscope, you can see the different cells in the plasma. They include **red blood cells, white blood cells** and **platelets.**

▲ *Three types of blood cells viewed under an electron microscope. (The colors were added by a computer since electron microscopes don't show colors.) You can see red blood cells, white blood cells, and, shown in blue, platelets.*

Red blood cells

The most numerous kind of cell in your blood is the tiny saucer-shaped red blood cell. These cells are red because they contain a red substance called **hemoglobin**. Their main job is to carry oxygen from your lungs to other cells in the body. Oxygen is picked up and carried by the hemoglobin. Blood carrying oxygen, or **oxygenated blood,** is bright red. When the hemoglobin lets go of its oxygen, the color changes to dull red.

Red blood cells live for only about 120 days. When they die, they are broken up in the liver. New ones are made in the **red bone marrow,** which is found inside the main bones of the body. Some capillaries are so thin the red cells have to change shape to squeeze through them.

White blood cells

There are several types of white cell, and they can live for a long time— some as long as 40 years! White blood cells are made by bone marrow, too. They help defend the body against disease.

Platelets

Platelets are very tiny cells with a sticky surface and no **nucleus.** They help to seal wounds, and are also made by bone marrow.

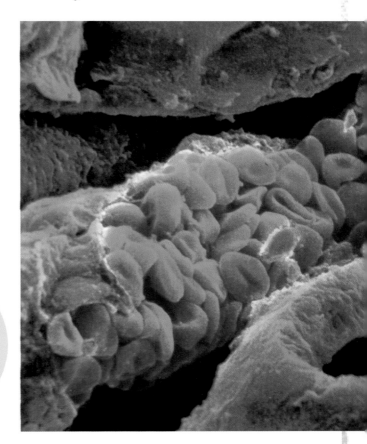

▲ *Red blood cells can change their shape because the membrane that covers them is stretchy.*

Heart Beat

Your heart pumps blood around your body. If you put your hand in the middle of your chest, just over the chest bone, you can feel it beating. It is made of very strong muscle called cardiac muscle, which never gets tired. This keeps your heart beating day and night, every day of your life. The heart is held in place beneath the ribs and between the lungs by strong threads. It looks nothing like the pictures on Valentine cards! An adult's heart is as big as his or her clenched fist. A child's heart is smaller—about the size of the child's own fist.

Inside the heart

When a heart is cut open, you can see a thick wall down the middle that divides it into two halves—a left and a right side. The heart is really two pumps working side by side. Each pump has a top space, or **atrium,** which receives blood from the veins. Below each atrium is another space, a **ventricle,** which pumps blood out of the heart and into arteries.

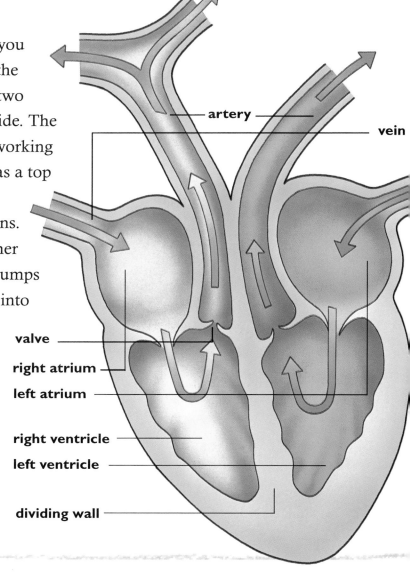

► *What the heart looks like inside. The muscle squeezes the blood in each chamber through the narrow valve. This gives the blood enough 'push' to get to all the main parts of the body.*

artery

vein

valve

right atrium

left atrium

right ventricle

left ventricle

dividing wall

A regular beat

An adult heart beats between 60 and 70 times a minute when the adult is at rest. That is about 4,000 times in one hour and nearly 100,000 times every day. During an average life, a heart will beat between 2 and 3 billion times. Children's hearts beat faster than adults' hearts. If you start moving, working, or doing exercise of any kind, your heart beats faster. This is because during exercise your body cells need more oxygen. Your heart must work harder to get more oxygenated blood to your cells quickly.

Supplying the heart

Your heart does not take food and oxygen from the blood passing through it. Your heart has its own blood supply—the **coronary blood vessels**. The coronary arteries supply heart muscle with oxygen and food. Waste is taken away by coronary veins.

◄ *A real heart does not look very romantic. It is a very powerful muscle, weighing about 6.6 pounds in adults.*

Did you know?

Animals' hearts beat at different rates than ours. Surprisingly, the bigger the animal, the slower the heart beat. An elephant's heart beats 27 times every minute, while in the same time, the heart of a canary beats an amazing 1,000 times!

The Heart Pump

Your heart is made of two muscular pumps that work together to push blood around the body in a continuous cycle. The right side pumps blood to the lungs to pick up oxygen, and the left side pumps this oxygenated blood to the rest of the body. Used or **de-oxygenated blood** travels back to the heart through the veins, and the cycle begins again.

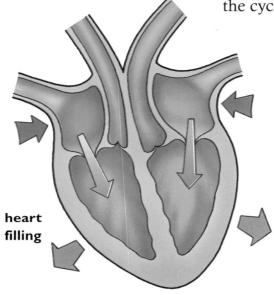

heart filling

▲ *The valves between the atria and the ventricles open to allow blood to flow into the ventricles.*

Filling and emptying the heart

Blood returning to the heart flows into the atria. When the **muscle fibers** in the **ventricles** relax, the space inside the ventricles gets bigger. Blood is sucked in from the atria to fill the ventricles. When the muscle fibers in the ventricles **contract,** the ventricle walls press on the blood inside, forcing it out into the arteries.

Tough **valves** between the atria and the ventricles and between the ventricles and the arteries stop blood from flowing back the wrong way.

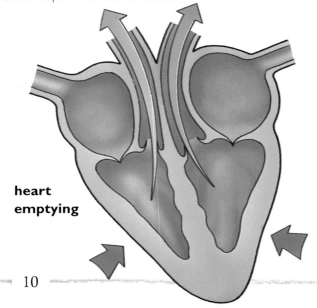

heart emptying

◄ *As the ventricles contract, the valves to the atria close, so blood goes out into the arteries.*

*◄This is an artificial **aorta** valve—it allows blood to flow out through the artery to the rest of the body.*

Valves

Heart valves snap open and shut. When they snap open, they let blood go through the heart in one direction only, from the atria into the ventricles. As the ventricles contract to push blood out into the arteries, the valves slam shut, so the blood cannot flow back into the atria.

Other valves are found inside the openings of the arteries. These valves look like half-moons, so they are called semi-lunar valves. Like the heart valves, the semi-lunar valves let the blood move one way only, from ventricle to artery.

Heart sounds

If you listen to someone's heart beat, you can hear a 'lub-dup' sound. The 'lub' sound is made by the heart valves slamming shut. The 'dup' sound is made when the semi-lunar valves close.

Did you know?

If a person's heart valves do not shut properly, he or she may get a heart murmur. Sometimes a faulty valve can be replaced by an artificial one. Scientists are now trying to use human cells to grow replacement valves.

Out to the Body

Blood leaves your heart in arteries. Your main artery, the aorta, leaves the left side of your heart, carrying blood rich with oxygen. It starts out about an inch wide but branches many times to form other arteries, which go to all the different parts of your body. The **pulmonary artery** leaves the right side of your heart, carrying blood that has no oxygen. The pulmonary artery divides into two branches. Each goes to one of your lungs, where the blood picks up fresh oxygen. The blood returns to the left side of your heart, rich with oxygen and ready to be pumped back out to the rest of your body.

Types of blood vessels

Arteries carry blood away from the heart, and veins bring blood to the heart. How does the blood get from the arteries to the veins? Arteries and veins are connected by fine branching networks of capillaries. Capillaries are very narrow tubes that pass close to every living cell in your body. The walls of the capillaries are extremely thin, so chemicals can easily enter or leave the blood through them.

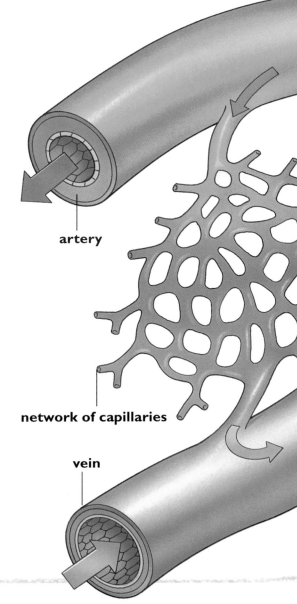

artery

network of capillaries

vein

▶ *Arteries and veins are linked by networks of capillaries.*

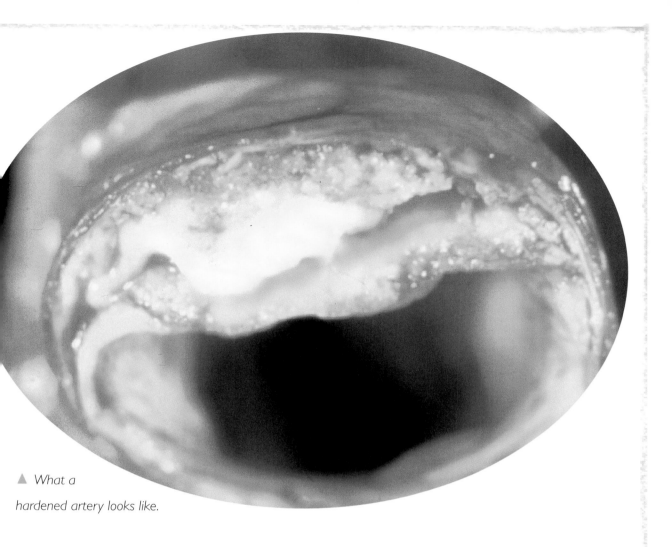

▲ *What a*
hardened artery looks like.

Hardened arteries

Some people's arteries become harder and thicker as they get older. This means the heart has to strain to pump blood through them. The hardening takes place in two stages. First, a fatty substance sticks to the arteries' inside lining.

Then the fibers in the walls become thicker and harder. What causes this is not known for sure, but doctors agree that following a healthy diet, not smoking, getting regular exercise and relaxation, and not being overweight all help to avoid it.

Did you know?

Water is what makes your blood runny so it can flow around your body. More than half your blood is plasma, and nine-tenths of plasma is water.

Back to the Heart

Blood travels back to the heart in veins. Blood from the body comes into the right atrium through two large veins called the **venae cavae.** Blood from the lungs comes into the left atrium through the **pulmonary veins.** Veins are not as thick and stretchy as arteries. Muscle action squeezes veins to move blood along. Vein valves keep the blood moving in the right direction.

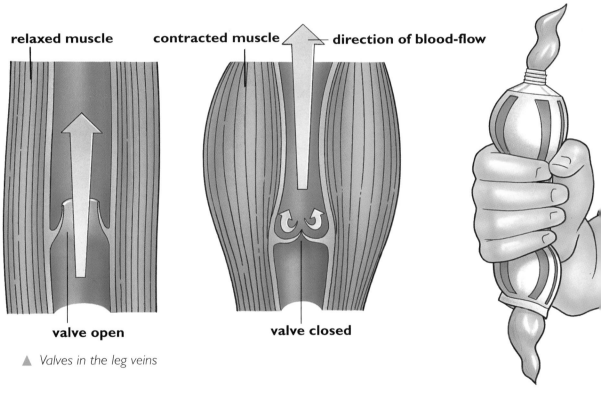

relaxed muscle   contracted muscle   direction of blood-flow

valve open   valve closed

▲ *Valves in the leg veins*

Vein valves

The veins in your legs and arms thread their way between muscle. As the muscles work, they squeeze the veins and push the blood along. Valves stop the blood moving in the wrong direction. What would happen if the valves were not there?

Imagine squeezing a tube of toothpaste with the cap off and the end split. When you squeezed, the toothpaste would squirt out both ends. The valves' job is to stop this from happening to the blood in your veins.

Varicose veins

Older people may get varicose veins when the valves in their veins no longer work properly. The blood flows back, pooling up in some places, and giving a lumpy appearance to the legs. This condition can be quite painful. You can avoid varicose veins with exercise. This helps to return the blood to the heart.

Hole in the heart

Some babies are born with a gap or hole in their heart between the left and right atrium. This means that oxygenated and de-oxygenated blood mix together, and some blood may not go to the **lungs** at all. Surgeons close the hole by cutting open the heart and putting plastic netting over it. A scar forms over the net and seals the hole.

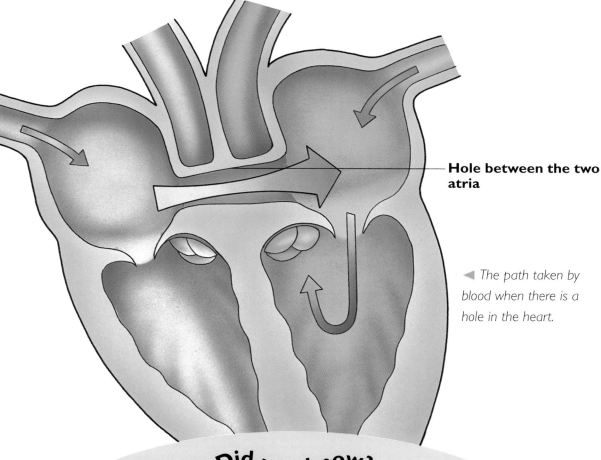

Hole between the two atria

◀ The path taken by blood when there is a hole in the heart.

Did you know?

A light-skinned baby born with a hole in its heart looks blue. In 1944 the first open-heart surgery was performed on a 'blue baby.' The baby had only a narrow artery connecting the heart to the lungs. The surgeon inserted an artificial tube between the heart and the lungs.

Pulse and Pressure

If someone has a bad accident and cuts an artery, bright red blood gushes out in spurts. Each spurt happens when the ventricles of the heart contract. As blood is pushed into an artery, its wall stretches. As the heart relaxes, the wall shrinks back. This bulging of the artery walls allows doctors to measure both your **pulse rate** and your **blood pressure.**

Feeling your pulse

You can feel blood pumping through an artery at a pressure point. Here, the artery lies close to the surface of the skin and can be pressed against a bone. You can take your own pulse by setting two fingers on the inside of your other wrist. Press your fingertips gently where you feel a pulse, and count the number of beats or pulses in one minute. This is your pulse rate. Doctors count your pulse rate to tell if your heart is working normally.

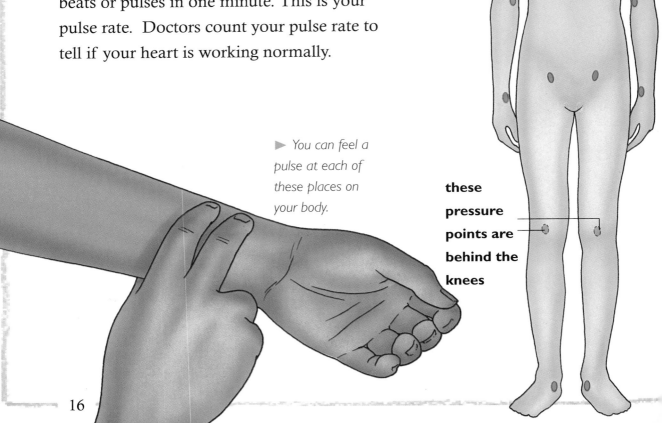

▶ *You can feel a pulse at each of these places on your body.*

these pressure points are behind the knees

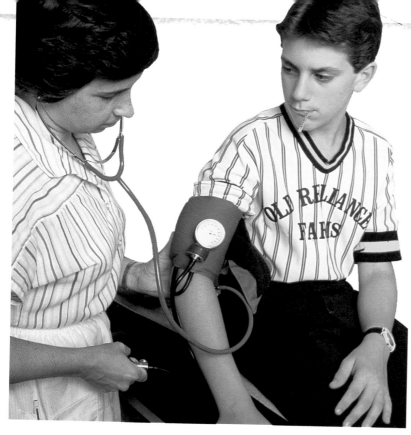

◄ A doctor takes a patient's blood pressure. It tells her how elastic the walls of the arteries are.

Measuring blood pressure

The walls of your arteries are elastic. When blood is pumped into them, they are pushed outwards. The strength of this push is your blood pressure. A doctor first measures the pressure when the ventricles contract to push blood into the arteries.

Then the pressure is measured a second time when the heart is refilling. So, blood pressure is given as two numbers—one for each measurement. A healthy adult's blood pressure is around 120/80, although the numbers will vary slightly from person to person.

Did you know?

When you are frightened or angry, happy or excited, your heart beats faster. You may even feel it pounding away in your chest. Your blood pressure and pulse rate increase, too. Because changes in a person's emotions cause changes in the heart, people used to think that feelings came from the heart. That is how phrases such as 'My heart was in my mouth,' 'He's warm-hearted,' and 'I'm heartbroken' began.

Pacemakers

Your heart muscle's natural beat is controlled by a group of cells called the pacemaker, found in the right atrium. The pacemaker produces a small wave of electricity that spreads through the heart muscle and makes the fibers contract. This electrical wave can be picked up by machines and recorded.

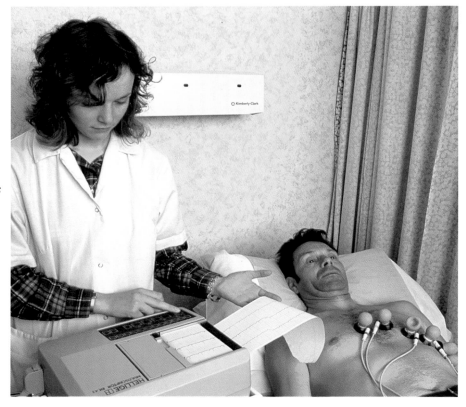

► *This patient is fitted with **electrodes** which pick up the activity of his heart's pacemaker.*

The heart's pacemaker

The heart's pacemaker can be checked by placing electrodes on the skin in different places around the chest. The electrical messages picked up by the electrodes can be displayed on a screen or they can be printed out and studied.

The device which converts the electrical wave in the heart to a display is an electrocardiograph. It prints out a squiggly line called an EKG. By studying an EKG, doctors can spot any problems with a person's natural pacemaker.

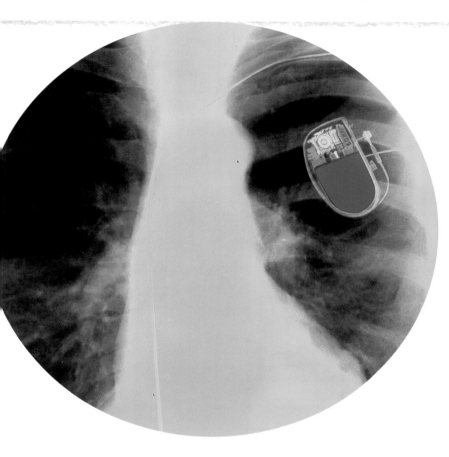

Artificial pacemakers

Doctors can now replace a faulty pacemaker with an artificial one. The first artificial pacemakers were so large they were placed on carts and the patients were connected to them. Today, thanks to **micro-electronics,** pacemakers are smaller than matchboxes and are powered by lithium batteries.

A pacemaker is fixed beneath the skin to the left of the patient's heart, where the doctor can get at it easily to change the batteries. A wire goes from the battery to the wall of the ventricle. This wire supplies a wave of electricity to make the ventricles contract.

Did you know?

Special detectors at the security area in an airport can tell if someone is carrying metal. When travelers walk through the security arch, a signal sounds if they are carrying any metal. Keys and coins set the alarm off, and so do pacemakers! People fitted with pacemakers are warned not to pass through these metal detectors.

Fighting Infection and Disease

Your body is continually under attack from microbes—**bacteria**, **viruses** and **fungi**—that may cause disease. To help you stay healthy and avoid infection, your body has ways of keeping these microbes out, and of dealing with them if they do get in! The skin, breathing tubes, and stomach are your body's first line of defense. If they fail, your blood takes up the battle.

First line of defense

Your skin is a barrier. It keeps out microbes as long as it is intact. Some parts of your body, such as your eyes and mouth, are not protected by skin. Here, tears and **saliva** can destroy bacteria. Your nose and throat are also routes into your body. Microbes may be trapped in the sticky mucus which lines the walls of your breathing tubes. Tiny hairs move this mucus towards the throat and you swallow it. You also swallow microbes in the food you eat, but the cells in the stomach make acid which can kill most 'invaders.'

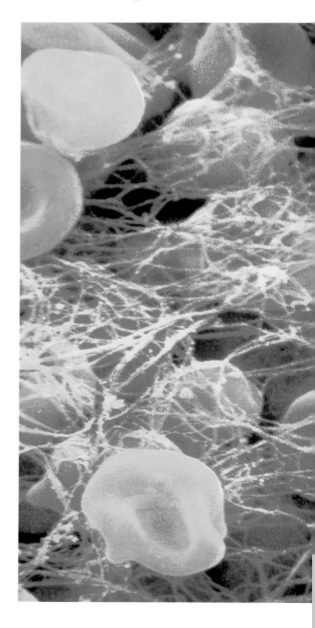

▶ *Red blood cells*

covered in fibrin—a sticky substance that helps form a scab

Reserve defense—the blood

When skin is cut or grazed, it opens up a direct route into the body. Even a small cut can let in microbes. Bleeding helps to wash out many of these microbes. White blood cells attack the rest.

▼ *A famous hemophiliac, Alexis, son of the last Russian tsar. Today, hemophiliacs are given **transfusions** of factor VIII, but there was no such treatment in his time.*

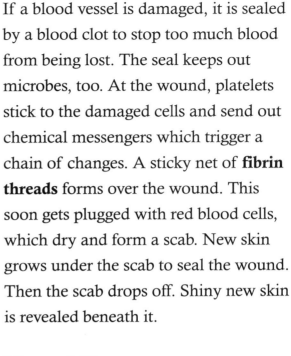

If a blood vessel is damaged, it is sealed by a blood clot to stop too much blood from being lost. The seal keeps out microbes, too. At the wound, platelets stick to the damaged cells and send out chemical messengers which trigger a chain of changes. A sticky net of **fibrin threads** forms over the wound. This soon gets plugged with red blood cells, which dry and form a scab. New skin grows under the scab to seal the wound. Then the scab drops off. Shiny new skin is revealed beneath it.

Hemophilia

The substances in the blood that make it clot are given Roman numerals I to XII. **Hemophiliacs** have no factor VIII, which means their blood takes a long time to clot. Any wound they get bleeds a lot and for a long time. Just the movement of their joints can sometimes cause bruising and bleeding.

Did you know?

Hemophilia *is a disease passed from parents to children. Alexis, the son of the last Russian tsar, suffered from hemophilia. Both parents had normal blood, but his mother carried the disease and gave it to her son.*

The Immune System

If microbes overcome the body's first line of defense and get into your body, they are much more difficult to deal with. They multiply quickly, and may even attack your body cells or release poisons called toxins into the blood. Toxins can damage your body and bring about disease. Your body has to identify the dangerous microbes and destroy them without damaging its own cells. This is the job of the **immune system.** The various white blood cells are the most important part of this system.

The body's fighting force

Some white cells destroy microbes by surrounding them. But if these white cells are overcome by the invading microbes, there is yet another line of defense. Other kinds of white blood cells recognize a particular type of microbe, and respond by producing a defense chemical called an **antibody.** This antibody fits around the microbe rather like a glove and stops it from doing any more harm. If this particular microbe has tried to invade your body before, the reaction is even faster because the antibody has already been made. Each kind of antibody works against only one particular kind of microbe.

▶ *This white blood cell recognizes the microbe as an invader. It therefore surrounds the microbe and kills it.*

dead microbe

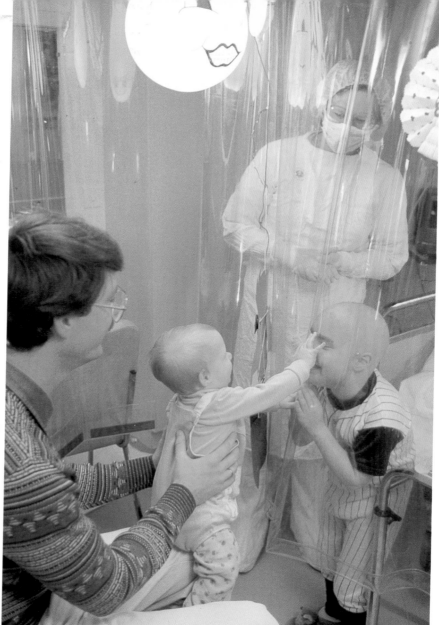

► The boy behind the plastic wall was born with a faulty immune system. He has no natural defense against infection by microbes. The plastic bubble protects him against dangers in his surroundings.

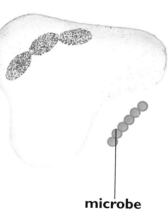

microbe

Did you know?

In the early 1980s, doctors noticed more and more patients with faulty immune systems. They were suffering from a wide range of very unusual infections. These patients had not been born with the condition. These patients were described as having 'acquired immune deficiency syndrome,' a long name which has now been shortened to AIDS.

Bleeding

Knowing what to do when you have a cut or wound can make all the difference how quickly it heals. It is just as important to know how to react if there is a serious accident and people near you are badly injured.

Minor cuts

You should wash a small cut in clean, cold water. If the wound is dirty, then dab it with clean cotton gauze which has been dipped in a mild antiseptic, such as iodine. The bleeding normally stops quickly. If it doesn't, press a clean dressing, such as a wad of surgical gauze, tightly over the wound for a few minutes.

Nose bleeds

The linings of your nasal passages have many blood vessels. Sometimes they burst and cause a nose bleed. You can stop the bleeding quickly with the correct treatment. If you have a nose bleed, lean forward over a sink or bowl to catch the blood and pinch your nose just beneath the bony part for at least six minutes. If a heavy nose bleed makes you feel faint, you must rest for a short time.

Serious bleeding

Losing lots of blood can be very dangerous. It is important to get trained help very quickly. To get emergency help anywhere in the United States, dial 911 on the telephone. While you are waiting, get someone to help the patient by padding the wound and raising the injured part. It is best if everyone keeps calm.

◀ *The correct position for treating a nose bleed*

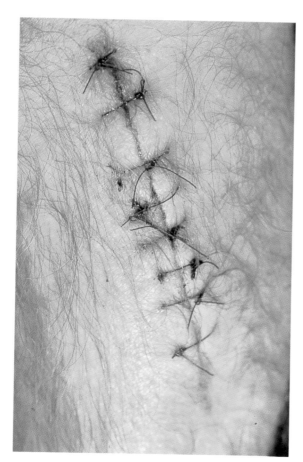

◄ These stitches hold together the sides of a wound, so that the opening into the body is sealed.

▼ Today, doctors act quickly to stop bleeding. In the past they thought removing blood, or bleeding, a patient was a good thing. They used leeches to suck blood from their patients. Even today, doctors may use leeches to remove blood from bruises near badly injured eyes.

At the hospital, a doctor or nurse will hold the sides of the wound together to help seal it. If the wound is large, stitches may be used to hold the sides together. A person with a serious cut should never be given anything to eat or drink, because he or she may need a general anesthetic. This is a drug used to make a person unconscious during an operation. A patient who has had something to eat or drink beforehand may choke or vomit during the operation.

Did you know?
Until the nineteenth century, doctors regularly used to 'bleed' patients with leeches. The patients did not feel anything because leeches' saliva contains an anesthetic that numbs the skin.

Blood Types

A person who is badly injured or has major surgery may lose a lot of blood. One-sixth of all the blood in the body can be lost without serious damage. If more is lost, the body will stop working properly. Blood is made inside the body to replace any that is lost, but this takes time. Blood can be taken from a healthy person (a donor) and given to someone who needs it (a recipient) in a blood transfusion. For this to work, however, the right kind of blood must be given.

The discovery of blood groups

At the end of the nineteenth century, when people were given blood transfusions, the patients sometimes survived and sometimes didn't. When the transfusions did not work, doctors noticed that the red blood cells were sticking together. The clumps they made clogged up the capillaries and stopped blood flowing through them.

An Austrian, Karl Landsteiner, wanted to find out why the red cells sometimes went sticky. He knew that blood always looked the same under a microscope, but he set out to prove that everybody's blood is not the same. He discovered the types of blood we know as the ABO groups.

▲ Karl Landsteiner first reported his findings on blood types in 1900. The first transfusion under safe conditions was carried out in 1908 by Reuben Ottenburg in New York.

Landsteiner's work

Landsteiner took blood samples from many people. He separated each sample into the **plasma** and red cell parts. Then, he mixed the plasmas with different samples of red cells. Sometimes the cells stuck together and sometimes they didn't. He realized there was a reaction between some plasmas and some red cells.

When the chemicals in the plasma and the red cells matched, the cells did not become sticky. When there was a mismatch, the cells clumped together. This is how he discovered four types of human blood—A, B, AB and O. Each blood type has a different type of blood protein on its red cells' membranes.

Blood groups around the world

The number of people with a particular blood group varies from one part of the world to another. About forty-six percent of people in the world have blood group O, the most common blood group. In Norway, though, the most common group is A. The rarest group worldwide is AB. In the United States, about four percent of the population have this group.

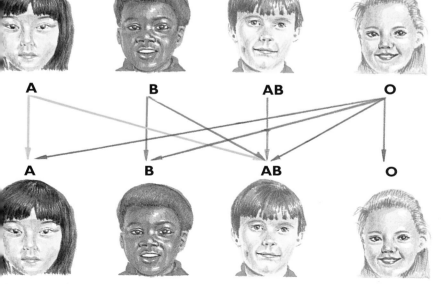

A   B   AB   O

A   B   AB   O

◄ *People with blood group O can give blood to all groups, but receive from group O only. Group AB can receive from all groups, but give only to AB.*

27

A Healthy Heart

Heart disease is the single biggest killer in this country. Yet much heart disease can be avoided by following a healthy life style. If you develop healthful habits now, you are likely to cut down the risk of getting heart disease when you are older.

Exercise

Like any other muscle, the heart becomes stronger with vigorous exercise. When you exercise, your muscles need more oxygen, so your heart pumps faster to increase the supply. A fit heart, however, does not have to work as hard as an unfit heart. This is because a fit heart pumps more blood with each beat.

Exercise also keeps your blood pressure low, as it helps your arteries keep their elasticity. To get fit, exercise at least three times a week for 20 to 30 minutes per session, to increase your heart rate.

▲ *Athletes are fit and have bigger hearts than most people because they develop the muscles of their heart with regular exercise.*

◄ *Being active helps to keep your heart healthy.*

Diet

Gaining too much weight is unhealthy: supplying blood for all that extra weight can strain the heart. Eating too much animal fat is bad, too. Some of the fat may stick to your artery walls and narrow passages, as rust does to old pipes. Hard bits of fat may flake off and form **clots** in the blood. If a clot blocks an artery in the brain, it can cause a **stroke**. If it blocks the flow of blood to the heart muscle, it can cause a **heart attack**.

▲ The Jarvik 7 was powered by compressed air.

Smoking

Nicotine, the main drug in tobacco, makes the muscle fibers in the artery walls contract. This narrows the channel through which blood flows. If this takes place in the coronary arteries, less oxygen and food get to the heart. If the artery walls have lost some of their elasticity, or have fatty deposits on them, too, then nicotine may block the blood vessel, causing a heart attack.

Stress

When you are excited or angry, your heart beats faster. This is not bad for the heart if you have time to calm down afterwards. But if you stay angry, stressed, or worried for a long time, then your heart keeps beating rapidly and this may strain your heart.

Did you know?

To help people with diseased hearts, doctors have made artificial hearts. The first one was invented by an American, Robert Jarvik. It was known as the Jarvik 7 and was implanted in 1982. The patient survived for only 112 days. Doctors prefer to use heart transplants rather than artificial hearts because they are more reliable. One day, doctors may use pigs' hearts for transplants.

Glossary

Antibody A defense chemical given off by certain white blood cells in response to the invasion of the body by microbes. The antibody stops the invading microbe and stops it from doing any more harm. Each kind of antibody works against one particular type of microbe.

Aorta The largest artery in the body, which leaves the left side of the heart.

Arteries Blood vessels that carry blood away from the heart, around the body.

Atrium The name given to the upper part, or chamber, of the heart which receives blood from the veins. The heart has two atria, one on the left side and one on the right side.

Bacteria Single living cells that function independently. They are so small that we can only see them through a microscope. There are millions of bacteria in the air around us and in our bodies. Most are harmless, but some can cause diseases.

Blood pressure The push of the blood against the elastic walls of the arteries. Doctors measure blood pressure as the heart contracts and blood surges through the arteries, pushing the walls outwards. They also measure it when the heart relaxes, and the walls spring back into place. Blood pressure is expressed as two numbers; 120/80 is a normal blood pressure for a healthy adult.

Blood proteins Substances found in plasma. They are also on the walls of red blood cells and determine the person's blood group.

Capillaries Very thin blood vessels—blood cells squeeze through them in single file.

Carbon dioxide The waste gas given off by cells when they use oxygen to burn food to release energy. Blood collects this waste gas from the cells and carries it to the lungs where it is breathed out.

Cell The smallest living unit. Each part of the body is built up of a different kind of cell. Most cells have a nucleus that controls what the cell does, and each cell is surrounded by a membrane.

Contract To become shorter and thicker. When muscle contracts, the muscle fibers slide alongside each other, and this makes the muscle block shorter .

Coronary blood vessels The blood vessels which keep the heart muscle supplied with food and oxygen, and take away waste products.

De-oxygenated blood Blood which has already visited cells and given up its oxygen to them. De-oxygenated blood is a dull red color.

Electrodes Devices which are used to conduct an electrical current.

Fibrin threads Sticky threads which form over a wound to trap red blood cells. The red blood cells dry out in this mesh to form a scab.

Fungi Simple plants that lack chlorophyl, the substance that makes other plants green. Fungi can cause rashes, allergies, and other diseases.

Hemoglobin The red substance found in red blood cells which gives them their color. It is the hemoglobin that picks up oxygen in the lungs, carries it around the body in the blood, and finally delivers it to cells.

Hemophilia A disease that is passed on from parents to children. Sufferers' blood contains no factor VIII, an essential clotting agent, so their blood takes a very long time to clot when they cut or wound themselves. Even a very slight cut can bleed a lot.

Hemophiliac The name given to someone who suffers from hemophilia.

Heart attack If one of the blood vessels supplying the heart with oxygen and food becomes blocked, the heart cannot work properly. What results is known as a heart attack.

Heart murmur A medical condition caused by faulty heart valves. The valves do not shut properly.

Heart valves Tough flaps, found between the atria and the ventricles of the heart, which stop blood from flowing in the wrong direction. They snap open to let blood flow from the atria into the ventricles, and then slam shut as the ventricles contract to push blood out of the heart into the arteries.

Immune system The system that defends the body against harmful microbes. It identifies 'foreign invaders,' and destroys them without damaging the body's own cells.

Lungs Two organs within the chest cavity that are used to breathe. When air is breathed into the lungs, the blood there absorbs oxygen from the air, and releases carbon dioxide to be breathed out.

Membrane A thin layer that surrounds different parts of the body, such as single cells or blocks of muscle.

Micro-electronics The design, manufacture, and use of electronic equipment using extremely small parts, in particular silicon chips.

Molecules The smallest possible parts of a substance.

Muscle fibers Thin strands of muscle which are gathered together in bundles. Together, these bundles form muscle tissue.

Nucleus A cell's control center, which tells it what to do.

Oxygen A gas needed by every living cell in the body. It, along with several other gases, is found in the air we breathe.

Oxygenated blood Blood that is carrying oxygen to the cells of the body. It is bright red.

Pacemaker A group of cells found in the heart which gives off an electrical wave, causing the heart muscle to contract regularly. The pacemaker controls the beating of the heart.

Plasma A yellow liquid that forms the basis of blood. It is made of water, with food molecules, blood proteins, and other chemicals dissolved in it.

Platelet A kind of blood cell with no nucleus, that helps to seal wounds.

Pulmonary artery The main artery leaving the right side of the heart. It divides into two, so that one artery can go to each lung.

Pulmonary veins These veins return oxygenated blood to the left atrium of the heart.

Pulse rate The number of times your heart beats in one minute. Your pulse rate goes up when you exercise, and when you are angry or excited. Your pulse rate is slower when you are relaxed.

Red bone marrow A soft, red, jelly-like substance found at the center of some bones. It makes white and red blood cells.

Red blood cells One kind of cell found in the blood that contains a red oxygen-carrying substance called hemoglobin. Red blood cells transport oxygen around the body in the blood.

Saliva The liquid made by the salivary glands in the mouth. It is produced when you see, smell, think about, or chew food. It helps food to slip down your throat more easily and contains chemicals that start to digest the food.

Stroke If a blockage occurs in an artery that supplies the brain with oxygen and food, the brain cannot work properly. The resulting condition is known as a stroke.

Transfusion A transfer of blood from a healthy person to someone who needs it, usually during an operation or after an accident, if the patient has lost a lot of blood.

Veins Blood vessels that carry de-oxygenated blood.

Venae cavae The two large veins that pour blood back into the right atrium.

Ventricle The name given to the lower part, or chamber, of the heart. It has a strong muscular wall to push blood out into the arteries and around the body. The heart has two ventricles, one on the right side and one on the left side.

Virus A disease-producing microbe that can be seen only by using an electron microscope.

White blood cells One kind of cell found in the blood. There are several types of white blood cell, but they are all part of the immune system and work to fight infection in the body.

Index

Further Reading

Asimov, Isaac. *How Does a Cut Heal?* Milwaukee: Gareth Stevens, 1993.

Asimov, Isaac. *How Did We Find Out About Blood?* New York: Walker, 1986.

Suzuki, David. *Looking At the Body.* New York: Wiley, 1991.